How to Talk to Anyone

Fail-Proof Strategies to Start and Keep the Conversation Going, Make Friends, and Build a Rich Social Life

Cole McBride

from various sources. Please consult a licensed professional before attempting any techniques outlined in this book.

By reading this document, the reader agrees that under no circumstances is the author responsible for any losses, direct or indirect, that are incurred as a result of the use of the information contained within this document, including, but not limited to, errors, omissions, or inaccuracies.

Table of Contents

INTRODUCTION.. 1

CHAPTER 1: CONVERSATION STARTS WITH YOU 7
  SENSE OF SELF 8
  BODY TALK 14

CHAPTER 2: FIRST IMPRESSIONS LAST 19
  INTRODUCTIONS... 20
  YOUR VOICE 22

CHAPTER 3: BE A LISTENER FIRST 31
  TALKING ABOUT YOURSELF 31
  ACTIVE LISTENING 41

CHAPTER 4: KEEP THE CONVERSATION GOING..................... 47
  MAKING FRIENDS.. 49
  FRIENDS FOREVER 53

CONCLUSION.. 59

REFERENCES 63

Introduction

If you hear a voice within you saying, "You are not a painter,"
then by all means paint... and that voice will be silenced. —
Vincent van Gogh

A voice within you may be saying that you are not a talker. It may accuse you of having little or nothing to say to anyone. The first thing to do is to silence that voice by talking.

You might say to yourself that you were not born a "people person." When you talk, you think you bore people (if they even bother to listen) and, to be honest, a lot of the time they bore you right back. People who talk to you never say much anyway. So, neither do you. You might wonder why, even though you want to talk to people, conversations seem empty, shallow, or stagnant.

You may be comfortable with certain individuals, but a voice inside says that there are people you will never be able to talk to no matter how much you want to because you are not interesting or attractive enough and they, being so interesting or attractive themselves, will brush you off. Maybe the voice is often confusing, labeling you as "too normal" and then as "not normal enough."

If anyone was socially awkward, it was Vincent van Gogh. He was considered by many who dealt with him to be difficult and contemptible, and no one could have blamed him had he decided to turn his back on the world and communicate with only his brother, Theo. Instead, he successfully achieved what he set out to do with his art, which was to convey his depth and tenderness of feeling to people, and to connect with them on a heart level (Wallace, 1969). His open, honest, expressive, and detailed letters to Theo have contributed to people's understanding of him now. He has come a long way from the fierce and unattractive man who often disappointed and distanced his family and upset his friends and acquaintances. Now people of all ages, from everywhere, strongly identify with him and are grateful to him for his contribution to art and culture. He signed his work "Vincent" instead of using his full name as other artists did (Wallace, 1969). His humility is all the more endearing to us as he is now highly esteemed for his artistic skill and his character, his determination, and courage. What made all the difference is that people now know him when others did not know him then. When we get to know anyone—*really* get to know them—we cannot help but start to understand and value them.

Everyone is interesting when they are honest about who they are because everyone is essentially like us, yet each person is captivatingly different from the next. We are interested in who we are and what our lives mean, and we are also interested in the different perspectives and experiences people have regarding this shared existence.

The truth is that we are all naturally, instinctively social. You *were* born a "people person."

There are ways that you think about talking and socializing that you simply inherited that are part of your genes and innate temperament. You want to use your natural strengths and weaknesses to connect with others without feeling threatened or as if you have to pretend that you are someone you are not. You do not have to be outgoing and talkative to be able to talk to people in a way that you find meaningful and satisfying. In fact, being outgoing and talkative can sometimes stand in the way of meaningful, satisfying conversations. Introverted and extroverted people are all social, but both can find themselves lonely in a crowd. Both can have deep and fulfilling conversations in the same crowd, strengthening friendships and forming new ones.

There are ways that you think about talking and socializing that you have acquired, some from stressful or traumatic experiences that have left you feeling nervous, anxious, and keen to avoid situations in which such experiences might be repeated or remembered. You want to be brave; you want to heal from past disappointments and hurt, but you don't know where to begin. It seems easier to stay cocooned, but you know that this is a kind of living death.

What you need is a series of fail-proof strategies, simple and practical, to help you be the "people person" that you naturally and instinctively are.

This concise and straightforward book lays out a set of strategies, starting with a chapter on bringing the key to a deep and rewarding conversation: you. The chapter centers around your self-confidence and how to come across as self-confident even when you are still working on it. It covers the way you look and the way you use your body to make an impression, offering advice on how to catch someone's attention and be attractive and captivating to the eye—and, by association, the mind— of the person you are talking to.

The second chapter will help you to introduce yourself and start the conversation, covering topics such as when to talk and how to talk (using your voice to its full potential). You will read about how to catch someone's attention, how to make them comfortable, how to introduce yourself in a likable way, and how to stay calm and concentrate on the conversation.

The next chapter follows on from this, discussing how to continue the conversation without awkward silences and dead ends, and what to talk about. Instead of putting you off of a conversation, small talk should be valued as the solid foundation of a genuine and worthwhile conversation. For a meaningful two-way conversation, you need to know how to listen well— without ending up doing all the listening!

The fourth and final chapter will focus on how to maintain conversations into the future so that people will want to see you again and continue talking to you. Throughout the book, there are many clear and useful instructions about what to do and, equally important, what not to do.

For a long time, I believed that I was anti-social and could manage with only a couple of friends and a cousin to talk to. As an only child of reclusive parents, from a young age, I was regarded as quiet and withdrawn. Often, I was silent even though I wanted nothing more than to talk to someone. Sometimes situations required that I speak out and, to my shame at the time, I did not. I hardly ever expressed my feelings aloud, even as they became more intense, serious, and sad, determined to cope on my own. Part of my inability to talk was due to my naturally reserved nature; part was due to formative incidents that shook my trust; and part was because I simply didn't know how to be heard.

When I was alone, I talked to myself quite freely; I think talking to myself did help immensely, but I ached for the fresh perspective of another. As I realized that people who could talk developed more connections and deeper relationships, I began to investigate how they talked by studying them. Spurred on by what I saw, I became braver and began to talk to them—a breakthrough in itself.

Much of what is set out in this book is the result of those observations and interviews. I have included two interviews to give you an idea of how they unfolded and how different kinds of people contribute to our understanding of ourselves. By the end of this book, you too will be a person whom others ask for advice.

Right now, a voice within might scorn that as impossible. If there is currently only one person in your life that you feel you can talk to, a voice within might say that there will always only be one and that no one else would understand. If you are comfortable talking one-on-one, a voice inside stops you from talking to a wider audience or in a group by saying that you will lose their attention as quickly as you lose track of your thoughts. You might have a circle of friends that never changes, and you would like to meet new friends of diverse ethnicities, beliefs, and backgrounds, but a voice inside says that you are not experienced, complex, or clever enough.

The voice within may sound like your mother or father or someone in authority who is just looking out for you, for your own sake, trying to preserve your dignity. It may sound a lot like your own voice, but it sounds like a voice with too much to say. It is a voice that *should* be challenged. It's time for you to drown it out with the sound of your own, true voice.

Chapter 1:

Conversation Starts With You

They may forget what you said—but they will never forget how you made them feel. –Carl Buehner

Do you find it difficult to talk because you have no self-confidence? Even with low or no self-confidence, you can talk to anyone.

The difference between someone quiet but self-confident, and someone quiet without self-confidence, is that the first can talk when they want to, but the second cannot. They are inhibited and silenced by their anxiety. They wish the floor would open up and swallow them, or, if they had a cloak of invisibility, they would disappear behind it and perhaps stay where they are; they want to be there, but without the anxiety.

By following the strategies in this book, you will wear the semblance of self-confidence as a cloak of *visibility* so that you can talk; and so that people see and hear you when you talk.

People with self-confidence are highly visible and seem to be exactly where they belong. Self-confidence becomes self-fulfilling when others expect it of you; you appear to possess it and they assume that you have reason for that. Your cloak, which is a state of mind, helps you to live as if what you hope for has already happened. It will help you to start conversations, thoroughly enjoy them, and make lasting friends. At the same time, it will help you to develop inner self-confidence for your deeper sense of pleasure and completeness.

Sense of Self

While self-confidence can develop over time, it does not necessarily do so. Children are often the most confident people there are. They are inclined to live in the moment rather than recall who they were yesterday and who they intend to be tomorrow. They often decide in an instant whether they like you or not and, if they do, will talk to you openly and at great length. The School of Life, which is an educational company offering advice for a more fulfilled life, demonstrates how children, despite having only a few years of experience behind them, are among the most interesting, or least boring, people there are (The School of Life, 2017).

It is as children become teenagers—when their brains undergo significant reshaping due to hormonal activity—that they become sensitive to social appraisal and seem to live in a state of perpetual embarrassment

(Somerville, 2013). How clearly I remember those teenage years of shame and agony!

But there are plenty of pre-teens who are shy and remain so, apparently reluctant to participate or receive attention. Often, their parents are also self-effacing; we wonder whether children learn such diffident behavior by example or whether it is in their genes. Studies have shown that there is an inborn propensity for the brains of some people, from the time they are babies, to be frightened rather than curious when anything new or out-of-the-ordinary occurs (Randall, 2002). I was such a child, and maybe you were too. It is unfair to expect these children to seek out new experiences or take risks as easily as children whose brains do not react in this way; but with reassurance, and by making the unfamiliar familiar through exposure, they can be encouraged to lead more adventurous lives.

Vincent van Gogh displayed great self-confidence when it came to drawing and painting and continued to work prolifically despite discouragement from critics and viewers, but he was insecure when it came to his finances. He avoided the subject to the extent that his anxiety about losing the financial support of his brother Theo may be what led to a devastating fight with his friend and fellow artist, Paul Gaugin; his subsequent mental collapse; and, ultimately, his death (Wallace, 1969).

As a self-confident person, you simultaneously: know yourself as a being of value just as you are, simply because you are (fixed); and know what your powers and abilities are and value them (changeable). Self-confidence is confidence in oneself as a continuously existing and fixed entity. You are always you, no matter how much you seem to change; even if you are disabled in an accident or by disease; even if you have an epiphany or find meaning in your life that you never had before. Self-confidence is also confidence in one's powers and abilities, which are fluid and fluctuating. Our physical powers and abilities grow stronger as we reach adult maturity; our mental acuity improves at a different rate; and when we are older, we are often wiser even though our bodies become frail. To possess self-confidence, we need to have a grasp of both the lasting and the ephemeral aspects of our identity. Some things about us are written in stone, others are fleeting.

Self-confidence does not come easier to the extrovert than the introvert or vice versa. At a party, the introvert may shadow someone they find easy to hang around with, waiting for a new person to enter their orbit, or even hide in a corner until a sense of inadequacy or exclusion forces them to leave, their inner voice saying that they should never have come in the first place. The extrovert may "work the room," mixing and mingling, enjoying the company of others while knowing that, when they are alone again, it will be with a person they hardly recognize or care for: themselves.

Self-confidence comes from self-knowledge, which involves knowing what your strengths and weaknesses are. People who lack self-confidence often exaggerate or downplay their strengths and often do the same with their weaknesses.

In order to wear self-confidence like a cloak of visibility, let's briefly discuss what it is made of and looks like.

The main element of self-confidence is calm. If we were sewing a cloak of visibility, the fabric would be a light and breathable cotton of calmness. Even when you are nervous, you can appear calm by relaxing your shoulders and holding yourself upright.

As a youngster, I thought that correct posture meant being able to walk with a book balanced on my head, but later, I learned a method of holding myself erect without appearing stiff or preoccupied, which I want to share with you now. By imagining that I was suspended from the sky by a strong cord attached to the top of my head, the rest of my body could "hang" relaxed from my head. It helps to concentrate on my head, holding it high, not with a lifted chin, but a lifted crown. The focus on my head, rather than on the rest of my body, also makes it easier to move my head around while the rest of my body simply follows in tow.

When you are calm and upstanding, you can look people in their eyes. Eye contact may seem scary but it is a way of stabilizing yourself by anchoring yourself to another who is receptive to you.

Breathing correctly, or rhythmically (not rushing or panting) and deeply (so that your stomach rises with the air), is essential to remaining calm. Regularly practicing controlled breathing will help you to calm your breathing in situations of stress and soothe your body into relaxation mode even when circumstances remain the same. Breathing properly slows your pulse, helps releases the right hormones, and supplies more oxygen to the brain (Stinson, 2018). For me, the four steps of "4-4-4" breathing are the easiest to remember:

1. Breathe in for a slow count of four (through your nose or your nose and mouth).

2. Hold your breath for another slow count of four (no inhaling or exhaling).

3. Exhale for a slow count of four.

4. Repeat.

I have used this breathing technique often, whenever I have an opportunity, but especially at times when I am tense and afraid; it always makes a discernible difference to my state of mind. Before speaking to a crowd, a while back, I felt my heart thumping and sweat breaking out on my forehead. Trying controlled breathing seemed difficult under those circumstances, but almost immediately, my uncomfortable physical symptoms subsided, and when I got up to speak, they did not return.

Other relaxation techniques learned in sports, yoga, or during meditative practices, will also help you decide to relax instead of being controlled by anxiety.

A good night's sleep is crucial to your composure the following day and the day thereafter. I find that focusing on the air as it enters and leaves my nose helps me to fall asleep.

Avoiding stimulants (mainly caffeine and digital screens) for at least three hours before bedtime improves the quality of my sleep. Alcohol may help you to fall asleep, but it ruins your quality of sleep. Since I stopped drinking, I have had more detailed, memorable, and meaningful dreams.

Alcohol is tempting when you are feeling tired or anxious about speaking to people and, at first, it may seem to "work" when you feel yourself relaxing and your inhibitions subside. It is generally our inhibitions that prevent us from talking, so when they are overridden by the effects of alcohol, we think that it has loosened our tongues. But the advantages are short-lived and, eventually, if you haven't become drunk and insensitive to the person you are talking to, overly confident about your newfound erudition, you will grow even more tired and irritable as your body craves a less and less satisfying refill. Rather try to replicate the first effects of alcohol in the way you handle yourself without actually having any of the addictive substance. Alcohol, when used as a social "lubricant," is just another way to sidestep and hide.

When you talk to someone, don't hold your breath or tense up but relax your jaw and imagine that you are expanding outwards rather than pulling yourself inwards. An unsociable person is fittingly described as someone "stuck in their shell." The cloak of visibility has no shell-like or armor-like qualities but is soft and loose. You have nothing to fear because your strength is deep inside: you do not need to layer yourself with protection because your core is indestructible. Your surface can be soft and vulnerable because, even if it is torn, it will be mended by the invincible source that is untouchable by all except you.

While the soft fabric of the cloak is made of calm patterned with openness, the detail along the edges is a golden filigree called joy.

Smiling shows that you are self-confident and self-assured. A genuine smile is the best sort and can be read around a person's eyes: even if the mouth were hidden, the smile would still be visible in the eyes. If you don't feel like smiling, try anyway; perhaps smile at yourself for not wanting to smile. As the corners of your mouth turn up, you will probably find that it becomes easier to smile and a false sort of smile dissolves into a genuine one with more ease than a severe expression does.

And there you have it: your attire for the activity of talking, whether you feel ready or not, is calm and openness decorated with a smile.

Body Talk

Once you have your cloak of visibility, you can wear it to maximum advantage by being aware of the body beneath it: your body.

In a society that seems obsessed with opposites, we tend to separate our minds and bodies as two distinct and divided things. We often think of ourselves as our minds and our bodies as something extra or the shells in which our minds reside. But science asserts that your mind begins and ends in the brain, which is a living, biological cell-based structure belonging to our body

(Crick, 1995). The first step in learning to talk is to believe that your body and mind are one, that you are not an abstraction somehow contained in a material shape, but that your thoughts and feelings are inextricable from your flesh, blood, and bones.

People with social anxiety often report symptoms of feeling disconnected from their bodies as they try to negotiate a social situation, even though their bodies are acting up and striking out with everything from sweating to blushing to shaking to having heart palpitations (Randall, 2002).

Having divided mind from body, western society has a history of further dividing the intellect from emotion, linking intellect to the mind and emotion to the body: "heads" versus "hearts." Intellect, seen as reason and consciousness, is often considered more advantageous than emotion, which is seen as impulsive, illogical, and subconscious. Although we know that most of who we are is subconscious, overseen by a relatively small segment of consciousness (Jung, 1988), we value the small, overarching segment over the immeasurably vast and fundamental one. We consider intellect more civilized and relegate emotion to an ancient primitive past. The word "emotional" usually has "suppression" following close on its heels.

Jaak Panksepp, the father of affective neuroscience, applied scientific research to the study of emotion, saying that we need to explore our emotions to understand who we are because they are not just "knee-jerk" reactions or conditioned responses to external stimuli (Leyh, 2011). Panksepp provided observable evidence that: one of our most sincere human desires is to communicate emotions; that we are built around and based on our emotions; and gestures and sounds can convey even more than words.

Last night, I attended a music concert in which a singer sang 'Parto! Ma tu mio' from *La Clemenza di Tito* by Mozart. They had rehearsed well. The singer obviously understood what the lyrics meant but most of the audience did not—not linguistically at any rate. They were all carried along by the facial expressions, physical gestures, and voice of the singer; everyone hung on every word so that, in the silences, you could have heard a pin drop. The singer's eyes glared into the near distance and then gazed into the far distance and, sometimes, seemed to stare straight at me; standing upright, legs apart and feet firmly planted, while the body slightly swayed, occasionally the feet moved to orient the singer in slightly different directions; arms at either side with hands hanging not limp but relaxed and ready to move, which they did as if in moments of extreme emotion, spreading outwards and once or twice clasping tightly against the chest. When it was over, the audience clapped and even laughed with delight, having been transported as they were by the singer's every move and sound.

The singer was also well-groomed and attractive, which added to the appeal.

Physical attractiveness can be subjective but there are generally accepted guidelines involving cleanliness and good health. You can prepare yourself for social interaction by ensuring you are clean, well-fed, well-exercised, and well-rested. You may associate these adjectives with a prized pet or farm animal but they are just as relevant here. If you are haggard from sleeplessness and worry, sickly, or disheveled, you will be less physically attractive.

Young people have the advantage of youth on their side. As you grow older, you can still improve the way you look by wearing well-laundered clothes, good shoes, and taking care of your teeth, hair, nails, and so on. You will feel happier talking with fresh breath and smiling with clean teeth than you will without, and so will the person you are talking to! How many of us remember someone fondly when we discern a pleasant scent that reminds us of them! Your natural clean fragrance (with a dash of fragrance if you like, even just vanilla essence) will add to your physical allure and contribute positively to your effort at communication. Being "dressed up" will remind you that you have taken the necessary steps to prepare yourself to talk to people.

Cultivate body awareness by taking mental notes of how it feels as you go about your daily activities. Walking is a brilliant way of centering yourself in your body and provides gentle exercise. As you walk, focus on the way your body moves, the rhythm of its strides, and the flow of movement from head to foot and side to side. Experiment by altering your style from a stroll to a march to a skip, and so on, and notice how moods manifest in the position and sensations of your body and how the body movements affect mood. Dancing is another way of directing internal, emotional energy into physical expression, giving the energy building up inside of you an outlet and release.

In summary:

- Remain calm (using breathing and your sense of belonging in your body).

- Maintain a good posture and an open stance.

- Make and keep eye contact with others when they are looking at you, acknowledging and appreciating their gaze.

- Stay centered in your body, using gesture and expression.

- Take care of yourself and be presentable and clean.

Now that you are radiating comfortability and joy, it is time to start using your words. Words carry just as much meaning and, in the following chapter, we will learn how to use them mindfully.

Chapter 2:

First Impressions Last

Go to the edge of the cliff and jump off. Build your wings on the way down. –Ray Bradbury

The best way to talk to anyone is to do so bravely, "winging it" as you go along. When talking to others, you cannot build your wings before you fly because every conversation is a slightly new flight with new wings. Every cliff is a different height and, after every jump, you encounter different currents and conditions that affect the flight and the type of wings that are required. If you bring ready-made wings, they will probably fail you: the wings must fit the flight rather than the other way around.

You will never be perfectly and utterly prepared for what happens in a social encounter, and to insist on being so will deter you from talking. If you try to recreate previous conversations or ones you have rehearsed verbatim, not only will the conversation seem stilted but you will probably be exhausted from the rehearsal leading up to it.

Initially, it may seem like a contradiction, but you need to prepare yourself *and* improvise.

Preparation, which was covered in the previous chapter, provides basic components such as the signs of self-confidence and the integral role of body language. Preparation lies in learning the basic mechanics of flight and wing design and obtaining the necessary materials so that, as you fall, you have something with which to build. Improvisation, covered in this chapter, keeps your talk fresh and lively. You will use it as you introduce yourself and decide whom to talk to and when.

In this chapter, I will discuss how to introduce yourself, spark off a conversation, and fan it into flame with your voice.

Introductions

There is always one person at parties who drifts around and introduces themselves with ease. People smile in their presence and become magically talkative. This person has mastered the art of introductions.

Your timing and your tone are important when introducing yourself. Being the first to initiate contact is a good idea, to assert yourself as confident and inviting. Begin talking with a bold, vibrant note, even if you bring it down right away. Varying your speed and volume as you move from saying something energetic to something more somber will prevent monotony.

A secretary once told me that she learned at college to smile when answering a phone call, even though the caller would not be able to see her face, because the warmth from the smile carries into the voice. She said that every time she speaks on the phone, she smiles, especially at the beginning of the conversation or if she feels the emotional distance between her and the caller increase, and immediately she hears a positive response in the timbre of the voice on the other side.

If you're not sure who to talk to, select someone free rather than a person who is already engaged in conversation with someone else. But if there is someone you want to talk to who is already occupied, making eye contact and using open body language will signal to them that you would like to talk, and they will probably come over when there is an opportunity for them to do so.

If there is someone in particular whom you would like to meet, and you know ahead of the time that they will be there and there is someone who is a mutual acquaintance, ask the latter to please introduce you to them. The mutual friend will probably mention it before the occasion to the person you want to meet and describe you in favorable terms, which will already prime the person towards you in your favor and assist with first impressions before they have even met you.

You can introduce yourself to a group in the same way you would to a solitary person, dividing your attention between everyone in the group while you talk. Pay undivided attention to the person in the group who is speaking, and respond inconspicuously with the rest of the group.

If you don't know a person, introduce yourself and they will probably reciprocate, but if they don't, ask them their name. If you forget their name, don't be embarrassed to ask them to remind you what it is. This will provide them with the opportunity to ask for your name if they have forgotten, which will immediately spark a sense of affinity between you. Remembering a person's name will garner some respect as not everyone can remember names. There are tricks to help you remember. One is to repeat the name immediately. Sometimes I am so quick to tell someone my name after they have told me theirs, that I forget their name in the brief interim. Instead, I have learned to say their name before I say mine or as soon after as I can. A person feels pleased to hear their name spoken aloud, and repeating their name during your conversation will serve the double purpose of endearing them to you and helping you remember it.

Your Voice

Your voice, when you talk, should be comfortably audible and warm, with a smile in it.

As part of my research before writing this book, I spoke to a Voice Specialist named Sarah Woodward (hereafter referred to as SW) at her home in Cape Town. She invited me to sit with her outside under a granadilla vine in her back garden, where we sipped wine, nibbled milk tart, and chatted while her husband planted sweet peas. There was a steady breeze scented with the sea, carrying the sounds of her children in the neighbor's yard where they were playing. What follows is a segment of our conversation relevant to the subject of "voice."

CM: You have a lovely, mellow voice, Sarah. Mine is also mellow, I believe, but it's not the first word I'd use to describe it. If I was comparing our voices to instruments, I'd say yours is from the strings—a cello—and mine from the brass. It's so different from yours—no surprise there, I suppose, but my voice is different from your husbands too. He has a very distinctive voice. I'd recognize you and him by your voices, only, even if I couldn't see you. So, the question that I'm getting to is: How does my voice embody who I am?

SW: That's a good question, Cole. Your voice reveals so many things about who you are. What language or languages do you speak, what dialect do you use—those are obvious markers. There are stereotypes about certain regional accents which we may have, and we may embody those stereotypes, or we may reject them. Sometimes our voices reveal our level of education by the vocabulary we use and the fluency of our speech. Yes, hormones will affect the pitch of our voices: you have more testosterone than me so you have a larger larynx, creating a deeper and more resonant sound. We could have an injury or reduced lung capacity and our sound is breathy or sounds weak. Our speech has a rhythm, sometimes revealing our inner landscapes: Are we nervous, cool, detached, or enthusiastic!

Here Sarah uses the rhythm of her voice to convey these emotions: "nervous" sounds hesitant and halting, "cool" sounds smooth and suave, "detached" sounds remote and disinterested, and "enthusiastic" is songlike and lively. I laugh appreciatively at her acting ability.

SW: Our voice can reveal our history, values, health, age, gender—you name it. The act of speaking reveals so much about who we are and where we are from that no wonder some of us become tight-lipped and self-conscious. We make snap judgments about people all the time based on what does or what doesn't come out of their mouths when they speak.

She goes on to explain in detail the physical process that creates a voice and draws the following helpful conclusion.

SW: The wonderful thing about the voice is that it is a physical process and so it can be exercised and shaped like any muscle in the body, so you can become more adept at using it. You can become more skilled at using the way the voice reveals so much about you to reveal the parts you want it to! It becomes another tool in the way you present yourself, like clothes or make-up, in my case, that integrates how you feel on the inside with how you would like to present on the outside.

CM: That is interesting, Sarah. It relates so well to all the other things about us that we can use to our advantage, exercise some control over, to express who we are, or how we want others to see us. Now, I've noticed that one of the main things that people seem to struggle with when it comes to their voices, is simply being audible. I've been at social functions where people seem to talk louder and louder, or the sound of the background music or other people talking seems to drown them out until they are sheerly exhausted from trying to talk. Also, some people just talk too softly. Many people are soft-spoken or murmur or mumble—teenagers have that stereotype attached to them. And when you speak too softly, you seem less confident, less communicative, and engaging.

SW: You absolutely do not need to shout to be heard. In fact, the more you try to force your voice outwards and away from you in a typical shouty manner, the more you will drive your audience away. The first tip is to power your voice from your diaphragm while bringing down your chin (this creates a larger chamber in your pharynx, which allows more sound). A good exercise is to try to say the word "hey" lifting your chin upward, and then again while trying to make a double chin.

She demonstrates, lifting her chin toward the rafters of the pergola under which we are seated, to which the leafy granadilla clings. When her chin is lifted, the sound is a little harsher and more strident. When she tucks her chin in to form a double chin, she explains that, apart from achieving a fuller voice, she is also lengthening the back of her neck and straightening her posture.

SW: We were also taught in Drama school to use the voice to draw people in. Most of the time when you can't be heard it is because the meaning of the sentence you are saying is not clear. So, actors are taught to fully align the intention of what they are trying to say with how they are saying it. Firstly, be as crisp and accurate as you can with your vowels and consonants. Daily practice exercises will make the muscles of the lips and tongue stronger and more accurate without sounding forced or as if you are overworking the mouth. You should never be working too hard while you are speaking. You want to focus on what you are saying. Save the "drill work" for "offstage": While you are "performing," you need to focus on your intention. That is a little hard to explain but, basically, it means matching your meaning to the audience. If you are in a room of twenty people, and need to be heard, you will need to use the muscles of the diaphragm to create a little more volume in the voice, but the main principle is to match your energy to the size of the room. Try and speak with the intention of getting every single person to really hear what you are saying. It's the same as if you are telling someone a really juicy piece of gossip; notice how you match your energy to the distance between you and them and how you speak really clearly so they won't miss a detail. A good tip is to imagine that whatever you are saying is something you imagine everyone really wants to hear. So tell them!

CM: Like gossip! I recently read about how important gossip is in human conversation, like grooming is for monkeys! It signals who your partner is, who your friends and enemies are, and what groups think is right or wrong in any given situation.

As if on cue, Sarah's youngest child, having returned from playing next door, runs up and climbs onto her lap, lovingly draping his arm around her neck and whispering something to her behind a dirty little hand. She smiles and nods and he scoots off again. I express admiration for her and the boy by meeting her smile and pausing to silently reflect for a moment on the charming interlude.

CM: Now, moving on, let me ask you: How can I physically present my voice so that people listen to me?

SW: Well, the most important thing is to be comfortable in your body and you need to figure out how to do that. If you're the sort of person who rocks from side to side on your feet, then you need to practice standing still. If you wring your hands nervously, shake them to release the tension. If you have ever been backstage before the start of a play, you will find the actors shaking and humming and loosening their muscles in order to release tension and appear comfortable in their skins. Perhaps you need to get used to the idea that how you present yourself is a performance and you need to rehearse in a private space. Once you are in front of an audience, or the person you want to talk to, a good tip for drawing people in is to energize the space under your eyes by thinking of your voice as coming off your cheekbones toward the audience or person. You are drawing them towards you, pulling them in, not trying to reach them with your chin and chest. A long spine, relaxed body, and slightly drawn-in chin is an essential framework to support the voice.

CM: Lastly, what is the one most important thing you think someone battling to talk to other people should do?

SW: So, I have spoken a lot about the physicality of the voice and how it is an embodied process, and there are physical things one can do to change the way you sound and the way you come across. Treat your social interactions like performances and do your rehearsals at home. Practice adjusting your posture in the mirror and strengthen the voice with regular drills and exercises. Practice reciting poems to your cat or monologues to your dog. The point is not to become a better actor—it is to become familiar with your instrument, with what you, in particular, are working with. You can't just expect yourself to be a smooth, confident raconteur (if that's what you're going for) just off the bat. So, get comfortable with practicing and rehearsing what you are going to say and how you are going to say it.

Sarah takes a deep breath and continues with emphasis.

SW: *Then*...When you are in public, forget about all your preparation. It is there, no need to focus on it. You want to be in the moment, in the space with the person or people you are with. I think a very important thing to remember is that people don't care that much about what you do or say as much as you think they do. Ask questions, be present and respond to what is happening in front of you. If it is a social situation, try and match your breathing pattern to the person you are with, make appropriate eye contact, and just respond to what is happening. Not that profound, but often very difficult to do.

As you see, Sarah suggested approaching the task of talking to people as an actor rehearsing for a performance. You might feel that the very notion of social interaction as performance and pressure to perform well makes you anxious; but remember that this metaphor appeals to Sarah because, as an actor, she loves rehearsal and performance. She gets butterflies and stage fright, too, but she uses the adrenalin to sharpen her performance. Different metaphors can be used to describe the "preparation" and "presentation" stages of conversation, depending on what it is that inspires you. A visual artist, for instance, could describe the preparation phase as the brainstorming and sketching that occurs before they start painting the final piece: A lot of initial work is never seen in the finished painting which cannot be too rigidly dependent on the preliminary drawings and ideas if it is still to have a liveliness and freshness to it. In another instance, a chef could describe the preparation as the effort they put into shopping for the right ingredients, the washing and chopping, the decisions that they make based on previous dishes they have cooked; the presentation as the serving of the meal when all the actions and methods leading up to that point are forgotten in the pleasure of smelling and eating the food.

In summary:

- Practice in private, then leave your preparations behind as you step out.

- Don't procrastinate, waiting for perfect conditions before you start socializing.

- Make eye contact with the person with whom you would like to talk first.

- Approach with a smile and use your smile to introduce warmth to your voice.

- Be the 'hero' by initiating conversation with enthusiasm.

Now that you know how to propel the conversation and make the person feel important, it is time to keep the conversation alive. The following chapter will guide you on how to remain present and actively listen during your social interactions.

Chapter 3:

Be a Listener First

A conversation is a dialogue, not a monologue. –Truman Capote

Talking is about more than words. It is about connection.

Even a guest speaker or preacher talks well when they keep a "hidden" conversation going with their audience by paying attention to it.

You have taken the initiative to break the ice. As the ice may form again quite easily, you will have to continue breaking it, to eventually get below the surface to the deeper territory. Small talk is more significant than you may think in starting a conversation and ushering it on.

As the dialogue progresses, you have reached the stage where substance matters. What should you say then and how good are you at listening?

Talking About Yourself

I have a handsome friend who talks about himself a lot so he has widely gained the reputation of being self-absorbed. He is an intelligent, expressive person and makes me laugh, but I began to think that he wasn't interested in me at all as he never talked about me. If he wasn't interested in me, why did he keep wanting to see me? He had many other friends. I wondered why he seemed to talk about himself when he was with me. He was talking because I was listening, and the more I listened the more he talked until this seemed to have become the motif of our friendship.

Then, suddenly, I found myself in his shoes while speaking to someone else, and it struck me: He was desperate for me to share more about myself with him, but instead of asking me directly, he offered all this information about himself in the hope that I would reciprocate. Unfortunately, it had been having the opposite effect, in that I was becoming more and more unforthcoming and even (I'm sorry to say) judgmental, suspecting him of conceitedness and inconsideration. When the penny dropped, I shared my insight without offense (because I no longer judged him) and he confirmed it: Not wanting to pry, he had offered me all kinds of personal and revealing information about himself to encourage me to tell him more about myself.

We cannot expect others to draw information out of us, but rather we should offer it ourselves. If, however, you find that you are offering your information and receiving none about the person you are talking to, don't worry about asking them directly whether they feel the same way as you do, have had similar experiences at all, or even what they think about what you are saying. When someone is under the impression that the subject dearest to your heart is you and you ask them to offer an opinion, they will feel flattered that their opinion matters and impressed that you are receptive to comment; they will see that you don't take yourself as seriously as they might have thought and like you all the more for that.

While it is important to share and engage with others on a deep level, small talk is often underrated, especially at the start of a conversation. Even firm friends will start a conversation with small talk. When it comes to small-talk, what remains unsaid shines through. Allusions to the weather or popular culture, or local and global news updates, stand for more than what they are as indicators of concern and desire for connection. Instead of despising small talk as shallow and fickle, see it for what it is: a gateway towards more talk. Someone willing to endure small talk is someone dependable when it comes to deeper concerns.

Small talk can include comments on:

- Your immediate environment or surroundings.

- Your relationship with other people there, especially significant people such as the host or guest of honor.

- The latest local or global news.

- Current music, film, happenings, or prominent figures in popular culture.

- What you do for work and/or recreation.

As the conversation progresses, appropriate topics will vary depending on whether the event is a professional or personal gathering.

At a professional gathering, there is probably a purpose to the event which you should support with what you say. It could have been organized for training purposes. Concentrate on what is being taught or learned and say things that are helpful to others in the group and facilitate the training. By asking questions and making comments, your participation will assist in your learning and others will appreciate your contribution and your courage to ask questions on everyone's behalf. It could have been organized with the objective of "networking." It is a good idea to, instead of speaking about yourself as you would at a personal gathering, base your talk on what you *do* rather than who you *are*. What you do includes your work or occupation, your pastimes, hobbies, your travels, and all that involves action and activity on your part. You can tell people about a recent project you completed or where you went on holiday and what you saw there. When people hear about what you do or have done, they still get a sense of who you are but it is based on concretes rather than abstracts. For instance, if you do figure-skating, people deduce that you are focused and diligent and agile and well-coordinated, but these abstracts are neatly contained within the clear mental image of a figure-skater.

At a personal gathering, you should talk more about who you (and others) *are*, which involves conversation around ideas that are more abstract such as your motives, attributes, and other theoretical qualities. You can tell people about how completing your recent project made you feel and what you learned, why you went on holiday and why you'll never go back there, and so on.

A topic you should probably skirt at a social event (unless the event is a spiritual or religious one) is religion. The other topic that is bound to get people hot under the collar and should not be entered into (unless the meeting is political) is politics. These two topics cause endless trouble in text messaging and lead to distress during face-to-face conversation, too. If you find someone with the same beliefs as you, you can converse with them to your hearts' content and come away feeling bolstered. But try to remain sensitive to others in your vicinity or within earshot who may have different opinions. By avoiding religion and politics at social gatherings, you may avoid inadvertent offense and hurt.

During small talk or talk about weightier topics, never underestimate the power of these two things of which every human is capable: finding humor and telling a story.

There are as many differently nuanced senses of humor as there are personalities. Sharply witty, dry, cynical, wistful, lighthearted, ridiculous, slapstick—most humor is very welcome. People at social functions are usually quite willing to be amused and will laugh at your slightest joke, as you should at theirs. According to French philosopher Jean de La Bruyère, the spirit of conversation is to bring out the cleverness of others so that the person you are talking to is left feeling pleased with himself and his wit and pleased with you for bringing it out in them and appreciating it (Damman, Antoine & Van Laun, 1885). La Bruyère was a 17th-century philosopher, but the sentiment remains true. However, one joke after another can become tedious after a while, so it is best to use banter or humor sparingly and vary the pitch of conversation so that it is not always funny but sometimes serious and not always serious but sometimes amusing. There are, of course, situations in which humor is not advisable, but you'd be surprised how welcome a little light relief can be as it offers just that: relief.

Avoid mockery. You don't have to take it if you try to talk to someone who makes fun of you for an impairment or disability. People who do so aren't worth your while, but if you still feel you need to talk to them, for some reason, involving a trustworthy mediator or third person can make all the difference, acting as both witness and moderator during your conversation.

Emotionally gripping stories, told from a first-person perspective, activate more areas of the brain and are more memorable than fact regurgitation (Zak, 2013). A well-told story contains an introduction and progresses with rising drama that reaches a climax and resolution.

I met Gerard Goodman (not his real name, hereafter referred to as GG) at a business lunch at which I was an uninvited bystander, having tagged along with a friend who wanted me to meet his boss and other co-workers of whom he so often spoke. I was mesmerized by his storytelling. As he talked, he kept looking at each one of us in turn, to make sure that he had our attention. He gestured with his hands and often lightly touched his nose or ear, which kept drawing us back to his face, which he didn't appear to do on purpose. He also frequently paused after an animated period of speech, as though to gather his thoughts, when he would often repeat a word or linger over it. He had a distinctive style of talking, not at all monotonous due to its fluctuating rhythm and tempo, but most of his success lay in his eagerness to keep us engaged. A month later, I arranged an appointment with him between his many meetings and, before our interview (which follows), I was astounded to hear that he had a speech impediment.

CM: Good morning, Gerry, and thank you for taking the time to talk to me. I feel that you have a lot to contribute to this book because, as you told me—and much to my surprise—you are a stutterer.

GG: Good morning, Kev. Correct, I stutter. I have a stutter. It was worse when I was a boy but I still battle to speak.

CM: Unbelievable. You seem so self-assured. And your work involves lengthy meetings and technically complicated but emotionally persuasive presentations. You've even had one or two tough interviews that were broadcast live!

Gerard laughs and shrugs, cursorily scratching his cheek and brushing a finger across the tip of his nose. He has a straight, firm-set mouth and shining eyes that catch mine for a moment and drop, contemplative.

GG: Believe it, I'm stressed out and I'm sure it shows.

His eyes dash up to catch mine again as he laughs and I automatically mirror his attitude.

CM: Not at all. I don't see it.

GG: Well, that's good. I've worked hard to make myself understood. There's a job to be done and I have to do it. I can't let a stutter get in my way.

CM: What work is it that you do, Gerry?

GG: Ah, I won't bore you with the details, Cole, but I'm a financial accountant. I wanted to be an engineer, but there weren't the funds to study that, so I became an accountant instead, doing my articles and earning a small salary to pay for my part-time studies. My stepfather wouldn't let me live with him without paying my way, even though he was living rent-free in my grandfather's house. My grandfather relocated and asked my mother to look after his house until it was sold, but my mother moved out and my stepfather moved in on the pretext of taking care of my brothers and me. I don't want to cast him as the villain, but he wasn't a nice man. I can't begin to tell you how much he's improved now that he's old. My children say he's loud and obnoxious, but I tell them he's a teddy bear compared to what he used to be.

CM: Tell me more about your stepfather? You mentioned that he wasn't any help when it came to your stutter.

GG: I think my stutter started when he adopted me, to be honest with you. Well, I was only around a year old so I hadn't said much yet, I was still learning and only starting to speak. My stepfather probably didn't realize how scary he was to a little boy. He's a big man with a thick neck and huge hands. He shouted a lot and smacked me and my brother, who is two years older than me, but he was softer on my younger brother who is his biological son. I didn't know I was adopted until I turned nine and my mother and stepfather split up. I was so relieved to hear that he wasn't my real father! Suddenly a lot made sense.

CM: Would you say it was largely anxiety that made you stutter?

GG: Definitely. And he was the primary source of my anxiety. The atmosphere between us was always tense. I thought he hated me. (laughs) When I tried to speak to him, I choked on my words and spluttered. He would shout back at me, "Spit it out! Just say it!" and cuff me. I guess he was ignorant and frustrated.

CM: And your mother, what did she do?

GG: Oh, she tried to protect me in her way. She had her own problems. But at least I could talk to her when we were on our own.

He stops, and lightly laughs again, but his face is alive with feeling. He goes on:

GG: I could talk to her. She loved me. And that makes all the difference.

CM: You mentioned that you worked hard to make yourself understood. What did you do? How did you "rise above" your impediment, so to speak? Does controlled breathing play a part?

GG: Well, I don't do controlled breathing exactly but I do cycle regularly. Early mornings and on weekends I'm on my bike, rapidly pedaling and breathing deeply. It definitely helps, and the sensation of freedom and excitement keeps me in the moment so that I escape the stress of other aspects of my life. I stammered for most of my youth. There wasn't any speech therapy for me during my childhood and adolescence. Nowadays, there seem to be specialists for every predicament. My own children, for instance, if they're not having speech therapy or play therapy, they're having physiotherapy or orthodontic treatment. It's a good thing I earn more than I used to! My mother, though, wouldn't have been able to afford intervention even if there had been any available. Although not everything has to cost an arm and a leg. My daughter's lisp was noticed early, and she went to free speech therapy at school for a term or two, no trouble. But I had to devise coping mechanisms, which I did, and my friends were patient with me, which helped. I think these days, there is a lot more awareness about problems like stuttering, and more people are forthcoming about it, so it's "normalized." If someone teased or beat up someone with a stutter these days, it's more likely than it used to be that other people would step in to prevent it and call it what it is: bullying. I don't always know when a stutter or stammer is coming, but when I start to feel that "trapped" feeling while I'm speaking, as if I'm not able to talk, I slow down and wait for a moment. Sometimes it's a long moment, and then I fill the silence with an 'uh' but I make it sound like an interested "uh," not a dull one.

Never a dull moment! I also latch onto the last word I spoke and say it again, sometimes several times, while I search for the next word.

At this, his computer starts to chime, signaling his next meeting, and he politely sees me to the door and thanks me for coming as he shakes my hand, smiling and maintaining eye contact in a way that makes me feel appreciated. Despite his tight schedule and high-stress occupation, I feel as if the time he set aside for me was devoted to me and that he was pleased to have an opportunity to see me again and answer my questions.

Active Listening

Do you really listen to someone who is talking to you or do you often forget what they said or have to ask them to repeat themselves? If you jump to conclusions about what someone is saying and pre-empt them, or finish their sentences for them, interrupt them, assume that you know what they mean, or tell them what they are "trying" to say, you are not listening properly. Telling someone what you think they are trying to say is not the same as summarizing what you think the person has said. In the former instance, you will be putting words into their mouths and making them feel as if you consider yourself better at expressing their thoughts and intentions than they are; in the latter, you are usually simplifying what they have said, usually using many of the same words that they did, making them feel as if you are still absorbing what they have said and going over it again for the sake of your understanding.

Active listening involves offering visual and verbal cues to indicate that you are listening. Nodding occasionally, gently smiling, leaning slightly forward, making eye contact, and mirroring the facial expression of a person talking to you are all ways of showing a person that you are interested in what they are saying and want them to continue talking to you, while fidgeting or looking away, at other things, are signs that you are not paying attention to what they are saying (Skills You Need, 2011). Have you ever seen a dog who is curious about what you are doing or saying to him tip his head to one side with his ears pushed forward? It is a very charming attitude.

You can improve your listening skills by concentrating on what the other person is saying, without pre-empting them or replying before they have finished speaking.

In western culture, people generally feel more comfortable with a conversation that proceeds rapidly and contains no pauses, even if this means speaking over one another to contribute to the conversation. However, many of us prefer a slower pace and a space in which to mull over what we have heard before responding. Don't hesitate to admit, "I don't know what to say to that," or "Please give me some time to think about that before I respond." It is also perfectly fine to refer to previous conversations you might have had with people and pick up old threads once you have had time on your own to think about what was said. There is no need to kick yourself in a moment known as *l'esprit de l'escalier* (French for "staircase wit") when, long after the event, you think of what you wish you had said during a conversation that has already passed. You should feel free to come right out and say it the next time you see the person, after reminding them of the conversation you were having. The thing is, they will probably be enthralled to think that you were invested enough in the conversation to continue ruminating about it afterward. If you feel the need to pause during a conversation, to think about what the other person has said, you can say as much and they will probably find it more flattering than disarming. We can learn from Japanese culture to regard pauses during a conversation not as awkward silences that need to be filled but rather as meaningful and courteous, showing that they are listening and would like the speaker to continue, that they are waiting for more information, do not want to interrupt, or are turning over in their mind what the speaker has said (Shigemitsu, 2007).

You cannot have critical and evaluative processes going on in your head until you have heard what is being said, as they will obscure what the person you are listening to is saying. Paraphrasing or repeating what someone says to you can assure them that you have heard them.

Two of my aunts, who are on good terms, overall, often end up arguing at Christmas lunch about the same thing, year in and year out. One is religious and the other an atheist. The religious aunt tries to convert the atheist, emphasizing how wonderful it is to be spiritual; eventually, the atheist explodes, declaring that she was born without the "faith" gene and will never be convinced of the existence of a higher power. As I said before, religion can ruin conversations, even between sisters. The rest of us used to get involved in the debate but now we move to another room and resume our festivities without them. Year after year, it's the same story. They will never resolve their argument because they each feel that the other is not listening.

When someone repeats what they have already told you before, it's because they think you have not heard them. Sometimes they raise their voice for the same reason—because they think you are deaf to what they are saying. They have not been able to convince you of what they believe, but more than that, you seem to deny any validity in what they believe. Instead of objecting, repeat what they say and summarize it in a way that shows that you "get" it.

People also seem not to be listening when they offer solutions to problems instead of simply empathizing with a person. When someone tells you about a distressing emotion—from trivial confusion to the darkest of griefs—they generally are not asking you to remove it but rather to understand exactly what they feel by clearly imagining it for a moment. By standing in their shoes, so to speak, you share their burden, and this is all they need from you—to validate their experience.

Timing, which you used to start the conversation, plays an equally important part in the rest of what you say.

You must be "present" in the conversation, not distracted or attending to other thoughts. You might think that no one will notice if you are not listening, but I am sure that you notice when someone isn't listening to you. You can do something about that, too. An intentionally longer pause than usual, while you re-establish connection through expressive eye contact and renewed warmth, will bring them back to you.

If someone is talking too much and you aren't able to get a word in, the two-way connection is faulty, and input is coming only from the other person's side. They may not even notice if you break eye contact and stare off into the distance. You don't want to end the conversation and restart it; You want it to flow. By using the strategies discussed in the first chapter, of asserting your presence physically and emotionally, you should be able to break their monotonous self-absorption and re-establish yourself as a pivotal participant in the conversation.

In summary:

- Keep and share your sense of humor and appreciate that of others.

- Tell first-person stories.

- Don't think about your response before the person you are speaking to has finished speaking, interrupt or finish someone's sentences for them.

- Ask for feedback.

- Refer to previous remarks or inquire further into remarks that have the potential for further exploration.

Now that you have the self-assurance to approach an interesting person, fire off an open-ended conversation starter and listen intently to what they say. It is time to keep the conversation alive and ensure follow-up.

Chapter 4:

Keep the Conversation

Going

Stay is a charming word in a friend's vocabulary. —Amos
Bronson Alcott

You may think that by having started a conversation by asking someone how they are, they determine where the conversation goes by answering bluntly or by providing a more in-depth answer. The truth is that you control whether the conversation develops well by asking the right questions.

Your reasons for wanting to talk to anyone may vary from easing a sense of loneliness to learning about other people, meeting new friends, and even finding a romantic partner or "significant other."

You may currently struggle to talk to:

- a particular person you like (you're curious about someone, admire them, want them to like you too, or you're in love)

- a particular person you don't like (there they are and as much as you try to ignore them, you can't) or one who dislikes you

- people who seem "better" than you (prettier, smarter and brighter, wealthier) or hold some sort of sway over you (a parent, leader, or someone who knows more than you do about stuff)

- groups (at parties, clubs, conferences) and people who are talking comfortably to one another who stop talking when you approach (or you're afraid they will stop talking)

- or people who are different to you in age, background, color, creed, and so on (you don't want to be unaware if you inadvertently offend them).

As previously discussed in the first chapter, your sense of self is impacted by your emotions. Sometimes we ruin our talk by overthinking it and doubt our innate ability by overthinking who we are or what we should say. We limit ourselves by thinking we're only capable of so much and no more or by sticking to our old routines. In this final chapter, we will discuss how to make friends with all kinds of people and how to nurture the friendships that you want to last.

Making Friends

"Forever Friends" may not always be available and may even disappear for periods of your life, but when they reappear, you pick up where you left off.

Some friends move elsewhere or develop interests that conflict with yours or just drift away despite deliberate efforts by both of you to stay in touch. It is a good idea to talk to these people when they cross your mind, by arranging to meet or communicating online with them. Even though you may seem to have grown apart, intermittent continued communication will enable each of you to reach out if you need to and just having them "in the background" will bolster your sense of having people to talk to about different things.

When it comes to people you like and those you don't, the best way to win them over is to convey to them that you *do* like them. Even people whom you don't like will have something likable about them and discovering what that is and working from there will help you to act warmly towards them and bring out more of the best in them. It is very hard not to like someone who likes you. Just as it is very hard not to smile at someone who has a sincere and sunny smile. You can get away with a lot just by smiling and seeming as if you are genuinely pleased with yourself and everyone around you.

After starting a conversation by asking a question, don't accept short answers but lure the person into providing more information. If you ask, "How is your day going?" and the person answers only, "Well, thanks," you could lure them in by asking, "So it's going as planned?" If what follows is just a "Yes," you can continue with something like, "Oh good. Mine certainly isn't!" or "Mine is too: I got everything done that I wanted to do this morning, including something I enjoy/have never done before/think you'd be interested in…" If the person says that their day is not progressing as planned, the next step is to ask them, curious, "Has something unexpected cropped up?" or "Sorry to hear that, unless something better has happened?" Other friendly questions that may elicit lengthier answers are ones like, "What was the highlight of your week?" or "Do you have any plans for the weekend?"

Your queries will show a person that you are interested in them, especially if you phrase them according to what they have already told you about themselves. "Tell me about…" or "I am interested in your…" are the first words in relevant questions.

Don't avoid people who seem superior to you in any way for, even if they are, they are worth talking to, and if they aren't, they are still worth talking to. If someone is good-looking, their beauty does not diminish yours; if someone is brainy, your intelligence does not decline. You should seek the company of people you admire and would like to emulate. Comparing yourself to them will kill your excitement and curiosity as you compete with them, feeling defensive and threatened by their success. Instead, celebrate others' fine qualities and draw attention to them, for which they will be grateful.

Make the most of learning from other people who are more knowledgeable or experienced than you. If someone you are talking to seems to be advising and instructing you too much, which will often be the case with a parent or a person older than you or to whom you may be obliged for something, assure them that you have heard them by repeating what they have said, even if you do not mean to follow their advice. When they are satisfied that you understand, they will move on with greater ease to discussing the things that interest you more.

If you want to have meaningful conversations with like-minded people, try joining a club or group centered around your interest(s). Sometimes you need to find your "clan" or "niche" to discover how easy it can be to talk to people. Talk often flows unhindered when it is done during another activity that involves a common interest.

Diversity also adds excitement to your life. Accept invitations to social gatherings that you would not usually attend and talk to people who seem very different from you as a way of broadening your horizons and adding zest to your social life. Ask friends to introduce you to their friends or use small talk to strike up short conversations with people who are waiting with you in queues. We can rely on our common humanity to establish a connection with anyone when we maintain an attitude of open-mindedness, respect, non-judgment, and ease. Don't judge or evaluate what a person says but rather try to understand with further inquiry and dialogue.

Talking to people one-on-one can be more private and intense than talking in a group, and giving up your time to one person shows how much they mean to you. On the other hand, there is a different dynamic in a group, where we get a glimpse of one member through others' eyes. Groups, whether temporary or long-lasting, should always be open to others, figuratively and literally speaking. When gathered in a group, keep the circle open so that there is always a space for someone else to join you. Be aware of other people nearby and reach out to them if they look lonely or you would like to have another opinion in a discussion. People will be grateful to you for including them. If you find yourself on the outside of a group or entering a room where people have already gathered and struck up a conversation, don't act as if you don't want to take part. Rather, insert yourself into the group, without interrupting the person who is talking or, if everyone stops talking when you arrive, greet them and invite them to continue with what they were saying. By wanting to join them, you are paying them all a compliment.

In a group, or when on your own, don't feel obliged to talk if you prefer not to. Feeling as if you have no choice but to talk is almost as suffocating as feeling as if you cannot talk. A quiet and gentle person is often more alluring than a garrulous one, and when they start to talk, they will often command more attention from people who don't want to miss the opportunity of hearing what they have to say.

When you want to talk, remember that small talk is a sign that you care about connecting and, as you try to deepen the connection, remember the entertaining and engaging power of an emotional story.

Not all social occasions will be ones where you intend to make friends; one day, you may feel the inclination to make friends and find that it doesn't happen; on another day, you may aim to attend an event for the sake of politeness, with no desire to talk to anyone for long, but then you meet someone with whom you strike it off and they become a lifelong friend.

Friends Forever

Timing is as relevant in closing a conversation as it is in starting one. Think of it as a conversation that is waiting to be resumed, that you should follow up on, especially if anything of personal significance was shared. Obtain contact details for people with whom you have a rapport and send them a short message when you think of them, letting them know that they have crossed your mind and that you hope they are well. Arrange to meet and, when the venue is your home or theirs, take it as an indicator that you are becoming firm friends. At your home, show them around your place; at theirs, show a lot of interest in where they stay.

Long-term friendships rely on kindness, intelligence, dependability, patience, imagination, and—perhaps most of all—maintaining a sense of humor which includes being able to laugh at yourself. Nothing binds people together like laughter, not senseless hysteria or mockery, but heartfelt, uncontrollable laughter that bubbles up between you. When you see an opportunity for humor, use it. My best friends have always been the ones who make me laugh. One of the main reasons a cousin of mine fell in love with her husband, and he with her, right at the start of their relationship, was that they recognized a twisted sense of humor in one another that they thought no one else possessed.

As humans, our social connectedness is one of the most defining, refining, and estimable things about us.

By the end of the second wave of the Covid-19 pandemic, I depended entirely on my immediate family for company. As we emerged from the second wave and were allowed to socialize again, to a certain degree, I discovered that I was reluctant, daunted by the prospect of catching up with friends and acquaintances and conforming to social niceties. For one thing, I would have to clean up my home before inviting anyone over. For another, I wouldn't be able to just launch into talking extensively about the writing I had done during self-isolation because it would be impolite and self-absorbed, but it was hard to draw my attention away from my writing after being so engrossed in it for such a long time. I would have to make small talk and fill my visitor in on what I had been up to during lockdown, as far as those activities might interest them; when I thought about it, besides writing, I had done nothing but paint the entrance hall and start a compost heap. Having stayed superficially "connected" with others online, mostly by scrolling through photos of their lockdown-inspired projects, I saw a contrast between what others had been up to and what I had done. I felt incompetent, comparing my ordinary life to the manicured lives of others, as social platforms inevitably lead me to do.

Suddenly, I realized that under the dirty dishes and laundry, and all my musings as a writer, I had buried much of my concern, care, and consideration for others, friends, and strangers alike. It struck me that not only was my self-isolation bad for me, but if everyone felt as I did and chose to stay isolated, the world itself would become a hard and cold place for everyone in dire need of kindness and compassion.

Solitude is good for a person but loneliness born from a sense of perpetual solitude is not good for anyone. Even people who are surrounded by other people and interact with people daily can be lonely if their actual relationships are not the kind that they would like to have. Loneliness affects our state of mind and leads to physical decline, making us depressed, affecting sleep, memory, organizational skills, comprehension, cardiovascular function, and immunity (Novotney, 2019).

There should be someone in your life whom you feel close to, close enough to talk to about anything, without having to worry about burdening them or being criticized. This person may not always be the same, but if there is no one in your life to whom you feel close, you need to talk to someone. This could be someone you think might not "handle it" because you might be surprised to find that they can; or it could be a counselor or therapist, someone who might not be personally close to you but who can help reflect you to yourself so that you have a better idea of who you are.

Friends do this by reflecting us, helping us to frame our ideas and beliefs by acting as a sounding board to test their plausibility. Putting things into words, to sound them against a sympathetic listener, can bring clarity and conviction, helping us to progress. Being a friend allows us to do the same for someone else to support, reinforce or realign them. Friendship is a space of connection, mutually and simultaneously beneficial.

To grow and develop as an individual, and make lasting friends who value your company, you cannot be too protective of your status or desperate to hang onto friends with whom you can't just "be yourself."

Individuals I have known as truly self-confident have always been those who do not care too much what people think of them. They care more about what they think of themselves. They do not necessarily always think well of themselves, or stay always positive about who they are, or feel that they are better than anyone else, but they do know themselves and do not expect more or less of themselves than they know they are capable of delivering. It is the people with self-confidence, I have realized, who are willing to admit their mistakes and apologize; who welcome honest criticism so that they can evaluate whether it is valid and how to use it to improve; who can clear misunderstandings and calmly hold their ground when they are misunderstood or overlooked because their own opinion of themselves is not dependent on others; who are pleased by another person's prosperity or promotion and do not feel that another's success is their own failure. In short, they have clear boundaries that define who they are. They may move them as they develop and mature, but they do not allow other people and circumstances to shake their faith in who they are at their core. They have personal integrity.

Although it is easy to envy someone who is bold and displays self-confidence in any situation, particularly someone who is the life of the party, ultimately, we desire to be someone whose honor and self-confidence emerge when it matters most.

I met a young man of sixteen who displayed this self-confidence when he declined to join his friends who were getting drunk together on an afternoon after school. Even though he was worried about missing out on spending time with them and apprehensive about whether they would include him in their "inner circle" in the future, he was sure that he did not want to drink with them. He did not like the effects of alcohol, especially as his friends became sillier, the more they drank, and he had his first match of the new season the following morning, so he wanted to be well-rested and strong the following day. He upheld his freedom to choose, content to leave his friends to their fun, without casting doubt or judgment on them. Instead of being pressured, teased, or labeled a "defector," his friends continued to respect and like him. What is more, one of them who had been ambivalent about drinking with them, felt freer to leave the gathering before he got drunk. Self-confidence liberates not only you but those around you.

In summary:

- Be prepared to like people and to show that you like them.

- Pursue friendships by finding out more about people and staying in touch.

- Don't act superior or inferior but show appreciation for the similarities and the differences between you and other people.

- See the funny side of life and don't take yourself too seriously.

As you try out the tactics in this guide, you are bound to be having more positive and successful interactions and deeper conversations. Your skills will bring you deeper connections. Before I leave you as one fully equipped to talk to anyone you choose, let's revisit the main strategies.

Conclusion

It's nearly impossible to accomplish anything meaningful and important in life without at some point having to meet new people, learn new things, and take on new roles. –Keith Rollag

The strategies laid out for you in this book are fail-proof because they are functional. They are simple and practical strategies.

You begin by thinking of yourself as confident, fearless, and social and you become who you are beneath it all: We are all confident, fearless, and social because, to be fully human, we must believe in ourselves *and* others. You are not alone. Talking to others is a way of connecting with them, a way of asserting yourself and acknowledging others.

Talking to anyone starts with you. You have your unique voice and your unique point of view—you have never existed before and you will never exist again. You are important.

Yet, when people try to encourage those they care about to "come out of their shell" or "live a little" by telling them how special and wonderfully made they are, their words can have the exact opposite effect of what they intend, making you less of a risk-taker and even more careful to preserve the good image that people seem to have of you. Sometimes, rather than build yourself up by inflating your sense of acquired dignity, it is better to hold onto the fact that you—and every other human that ever existed—must make embarrassing mistakes if you are going to try to live to your full potential (The School of Life, 2017). Never forget this, and never forget that it applies to everyone. We are all equally important and equally foolish.

Our importance is not relative to our foolishness: no matter how we embarrass ourselves, we remain immensely important, and it is in this importance that our inherent, endless dignity lies.

You can even strike up a conversation with that certain person you thought you would never be able to talk to. You can talk to *anyone*.

In a crowd, people see you as self-assured, belonging there because you belong wherever you are. Your inviting demeanor that says, "Let's talk!" before you have said a word. You know that you have something to say.

You can choose anyone you feel motivated to talk to and, looking calm and composed, you make eye-contact with them, demonstrating an attitude of openness. Your heart may pound, and you may need to take a deep breath, but, before you know it, the worst will be over because you'll have taken the next step of talking to them as if you are not afraid.

Your standards for yourself and others are not demanding; rather, you expect the best of others and give them the benefit of the doubt, and you don't criticize yourself and others unless it is with forgiveness close at hand. People identify with you and you with them. You are a hero for being the first to spark a conversation.

You remember not to take yourself (or other people) too seriously. You don't lose your sense of humor because nothing diffuses tension like a laugh. If you are still too self-conscious to make jokes, you smile and appreciate the jokes told by others.

As you internalize the tips in this book, you will transform. The more you apply the strategies in this book, the more intuitive they will become. My main objective is for you to become so accustomed to them that by the time you have played the role of "yourself talking to anyone," you will define the role and live it.

It was in my twenties that I wondered how to continue living as an "outsider," outside of anyone else's thoughts and memories. I thought that I was alone, desolate, and meant nothing to anyone. It wasn't true but the "the voice within," when it brings you down and makes you its slave, is a liar. Thankfully my desire to be missed made me think again and search for infallible answers. Life has meaning for me in that being human has meaning. A large aspect of that is what I have in common with other humans and how I form lasting bonds with them. My loneliness almost drove me to despair but, at my lowest point, I stopped resenting people who seemed comfortable enough in their skins to talk to anyone (even me) and started reaching out to them. Pleased, many of them became so invested in me that they deliberately but subtly included me in their future conversations. I realized that they were doing for me what my parents would have had they had more confidence themselves.

Life is too brief and precious to be stunted by the prospect of failure. The worst that could happen is that you embarrass yourself or someone else when you talk. This is less of a failure than not taking the risk and obeying an impulse disguised as "the voice within" that compels you to preserve your dignity at all costs, even the cost of your own vitality and joy. Everyone is familiar with embarrassment: humans are inclined to make mistakes. Most mistakes have the advantage of bringing insight and opportunity with them. Making apologies, and accepting apologies, are never signs of weakness but of strength.

You know that after you have talked to whomever it is you want to talk to, you will take away from the experience something that made you grow as a person, even when conversations are difficult. You know that you can look back on the conversation and say, "I did it." You are the instigator and facilitator of the conversations you want to have.

You cannot fail when using the strategies in this book because by using them you are saying "Yes" to connectedness with other human beings who matter to you—to a fuller, better life as you.

If you still doubt your ability to talk to anyone, please read this book again (or parts of it). It might even be funny to refer to it in an icebreaker: "I read a book 'How to Talk to Anyone' and I've decided to talk to you."

References

Alcott, A. B. (1872). *Concord days*. Roberts Brothers.

Carl Gustav Jung. (1988). *On The Nature Of The Psyche*. Ark Paperbacks.

Crick, F. (1995). *The Astonishing Hypothesis: The Scientific Search For The Soul*. Simon & Schuster.

De, J., Damman, B., Antoine, J., & Henri Van Laun. (1885). **The "Characters" of Jean de La Bruyère**. Scribner & Welford.

Evans, R. L. (1976). *Richard Evans' Quote Book*. Publishers Press.

Leyh, A. (2011, June). *Why do rats laugh? Interview with Jaak Panksepp*. [Video] Braincast. https://scilogs.spektrum.de/braincast/systems-of-emotions-1-video/

Merriam-Webster. (2022). *Merriam-Webster dictionary*. Merriam-Webster.com. https://www.merriam-webster.com/

Novotney, A. (2019, May). *The risks of social isolation*. American Psychological Association.

https://www.apa.org/monitor/2019/05/ce-corner-isolation

Randall, T. (Director). (2002, April 22). *Afraid of People*. [Documentary]. Freedom from Fear & Randall Productions.

Shigemitsu, Y. (2007). *A pause in conversation for Japanese native speakers: a case study of successful and unsuccessful conversation in terms of pause through intercultural communication.* Core. https://core.ac.uk/download/pdf/234015866.pdf

Skillsyouneed. (2011). *Active listening.* Skillsyouneed.com. https://www.skillsyouneed.com/ips/active-listening.html

Somerville, L. H. (2013). *The Teenage Brain.* Current Directions in Psychological Science, 22(2), 121–127. https://doi.org/10.1177/0963721413476512

Stinson, A. (2018, June 1). *Box breathing: how to do it, benefits, and tips.* Www.medicalnewstoday.com. https://www.medicalnewstoday.com/articles/321805#why-breath-is-vital-to-health

The School of Life. (2017a, January 30). *How not to be boring.* Www.youtube.com. https://www.youtube.com/watch?v=M9i2HAE-ZSw

The School of Life. (2017b, February 8). *How to be confident.* Www.youtube.com. https://www.youtube.com/watch?v=0Tk82hE HNnY

The School of Life. (2022, March 2). *How to be an interesting person.* Www.youtube.com. https://www.youtube.com/watch?v=j0wBQA3 fOcg

Wallace, R., & Time-Life Books. (1969). *The World of van Gogh : 1853-1890.* Time-Life Books.

Zak, P. (2013, December 17). *How stories change the brain.* Greater Good. https://greatergood.berkeley.edu/article/item/ how_stories_change_brain